WHILE I AM DRAWING BREATH

Rose Ausländer
WHILE I AM DRAWING BREATH

cs

Translated by Anthony Vivis
& Jean Boase-Beier

PUBLICATIONS
2014

Published by Arc Publications
Nanholme Mill, Shaw Wood Road
Todmorden OL14 6DA, UK
www.arcpublications.co.uk

Original poems by Rose Ausländer
© Rose Ausländer Stiftung, 2014
Translation copyright © Jean Boase-Beier & Anthony Vivis, 2014
Introduction copyright © Jean Boase-Beier & Anthony Vivis, 2014
Copyright in the present edition © Arc Publications, 2014

Design by Tony Ward
Printed in Great Britain by TJ International,
Padstow, Cornwall

978 1906570 30 9 (pbk)
978 1906570 31 6 (hbk)

ACKNOWLEDGEMENTS
The poems in the original German are reproduced by
permission of S. Fischer Verlag GmbH,
Frankfurt am Main, Germany.

Supported using public funding by
ARTS COUNCIL
ENGLAND
LOTTERY FUNDED

**'Arc Classics:
NewTranslations of Great Poets of the Past'
Series Editor: Jean Boase-Beier**

CONTENTS

*This volume is dedicated to
the memory of*

Anthony Vivis

1943-2013

Rose Ausländer was born in 1901 in the city of Czernowitz in the Carpathian foothills, in what was then part of Austria-Hungary, to German-speaking Jewish parents. She was to lead a very unsettled life, fleeing occupation and persecution, living alternately in America and in Europe, writing partly in German and partly in English. There were, however, elements of stability in this uneasy life. One was poetry itself and the writing of poetry. So it is not surprising that a constant theme of her poems is words, and the power of words. She celebrates "weavers of words" ('Dust the Joins' p. 21), who are free to believe in their value and their healing power, in the power of the imagination, those who "fly to the stars".

Her childhood in Czernowitz, a town with a full and rich cultural life, was very happy, if perhaps somewhat over-protected. The initial upheaval came during the First World War, when the family was forced to flee, first to Vienna and later to Budapest, to escape the Romanian occupation. Many of her poems reflect the happiness and the mysteries of childhood; she writes, though, not only of fairies and nymphs, but also of dragons. The poems express joy and security: "sleep yourself awake / my child / I will light your way" ('Your House' p. 73), but often in the same breath there is fear and misery, the pain of the "children who played in the fire" (p. 73). Typically, in 'Snow' (p. 51), the childhood figures of Snow White and the Seven Dwarves appear, but in the background "beyond the mountains" there is the threatening presence of the "dark queen", who follows Snow White as inevitably as night comes after day.

After the war, Czernowitz became part of Romania, and the family returned. Rose studied Philosophy and Literature at Czernowitz University and became familiar with the literature of Goethe, Hölderlin, Trakl and Kafka,

11

as well as with the philosophy of Plato and Spinoza, and of Constantin Brunner, with whom she was to exchange many letters.

In 1921, after her father's death had brought financial hardship upon the family, Rose and her friend Ignaz Ausländer emigrated to America. They married in 1923 in New York. It was at this time that her first poems were published in anthologies. After seven years of marriage, the couple divorced, and Rose Ausländer returned to Czernowitz, as she was to do many times during her life. Her poems were published there in a number of anthologies and literary journals. A first collection, *Der Regenbogen* (The Rainbow), appeared in 1939, receiving good reviews. But it was not particularly successful. As a Jewish writer, Rose Ausländer was treated with contempt in Germany and Austria. She again went to live in the USA because of the vulnerable situation of the Jews in Eastern Europe, but her mother's illness prompted her to return almost immediately. She took work in a factory, continuing to write poetry throughout this time, and in fact, as many writers in similar circumstances have found, her writing provided her with a sense of stability and perhaps of transcendence. In 1941, when Czernowitz was occupied by the Nazis, she and her family were sent to live in the Jewish ghetto. For more than a year, she and her mother were forced to hide, moving from cellar to cellar, helped by courageous friends. She continued to write poetry. And at this time she first met Paul Antschel, who was later to call himself Paul Celan.

The hardships of a life in hiding, the constant fear of Nazi terror, the horror of the concentration camps are all present in her many poems which speak, often indirectly, of those years. These poems are filled with images of hunger and poverty, of wounds, blood, coffins, fire and ashes, smoke.

Other poems speak, again indirectly, of the mother for whose sake she endured these hardships. In later poems, the mother becomes a symbol for the air we are destroying, the "essential mother" (p. 47), or for the healing power of language: "mother tongue / you piece me together" (p. 21).

The ghetto in Czernowitz was liberated by the Russians in 1944, but life was not easy for the German-speaking Jews, many of whom were now subjected to terrible persecution by their "liberators". Rose Ausländer was comparatively lucky, finding work in a library, and managing to make contact with many writers as part of a literary circle. In 1946, the Northern part of Bukovina, including Czernowitz, became part of Ukraine. That year, she left for New York. Her health was very poor, and she suffered a complete breakdown when her mother, for whom she had been trying to obtain a visa to join her in New York, died in 1947.

For the next few years, as she tried to come to terms with her mother's death, she rejected her mother tongue, writing no more in German but publishing many poems and translations in English. It was not until ten years after her mother's death that, having visited Europe in the meantime and revived her friendship with Paul Celan, she started to write in German again, changing her poetic style quite radically. Partly as a result of the influence of Celan's work, she abandoned the strict rhyme schemes and metrical patterns of her earlier work for a freer but more compressed style. It is to these later poems, written after a long silence in her mother tongue, that most of those collected here belong. Full rhyme has now frequently given way to less obvious assonance and alliteration, and strict metre to the rhythms of colloquial speech. As

13

in her earlier poems, there is a complete absence of punct-
uation, giving scope for multiple interpretation. It is this
later style which has come, in German-speaking coun-
tries, to be most closely associated with the work of Rose
Ausländer. An example is 'Mühlen aus Wind' (p. 74):

Das tägliche Brot
kommt uns teuer zu stehen

Mühlen aus Wind
mahlen Sandmehl

Am Rand einer Rinde
ernährt sich
die Not

Gib was du nicht hast
Liebe dem Nachbarn

Was suchst du
im flüchtenden Wasser
Narziß

There is a tight, though unobtrusive, structure of syntac-
tic patterning in this poem. The repetition of the etymo-
logically related *Mühlen, mahlen, -mehl* gives iconic force
to the description of a mill turning. The slant-rhyme of
Rand – Rinde, the full rhyme of *Brot – Not* underline this
repetitive structure which represents not just the turning
of a mill but an associated lack of progression which itself
echoes the negative circular hollowness of mills which
are not driven by wind but are actually made of it, of fam-
ine which feeds where people do not, of non-existent love,
of only oneself mirrored in the water.

A poem like this seems simple, almost cosy at first
glance. But the comforting images of daily bread, mills,

flower, water are used as vehicles to speak of famine, deprivation, lack of love, self-obsession. It is this juxtaposition of the everyday, the colloquial, with an unexpected subtle menace which gives the poems their power to unsettle. It is also this very juxtaposition which renders the translator's task so difficult. The lexis must be kept simple; these are threats inherent in everyday life. It is difficult, though, to recreate a repetition like Mühlen, mahlen, -mehl in a language which renders them as non-alliterating mills, grind, flour. Here is our version (p. 75):

Our daily bread
comes at great cost

Mills made of wind
grind the grains of sand

Famine feeds
on the edge
of a crust

Give your neighbour the love
you have never had

What is it you are seeking
in the fleeting water
Narcissus

Here *mills* has been made to alliterate with *made, grind* with *grains,* and half-rhyme has been added in *wind, grind,* and *sand* to preserve at least some of the circular monotony. The alliteration of *Am Rand einer Rinde* has been echoed in *famine feeds,* and the rhyme of *Brot* and *Not,* which in the German serves to emphasise their contrasting nature, is at least partially captured in *cost* and *crust,* slant rhymes which also fall on contrasting concepts.

15

In many of her later poems Ausländer uses this combination of repetitive phonetic (and often also syntactic) patterning with simple vocabulary and contrasting concepts. She also develops the use of key words which run like a thread through all her later work: dream, breath, gold, white, crystal, stars, ashes.

In 1965 Rose Ausländer returned for the final time to Europe, living in Düsseldorf and travelling a great deal. Her second collection of poetry, *Blinder Sommer* (Blind Summer), appeared that year. Though it received one or two excellent reviews, it did not reach a large audience. Greater fame came with her third collection, *36 Gerechte* (36 of The Just), published in 1967. Her work began to be widely anthologised and she received a number of literary prizes.

After this, many collections of her poetry appeared, bringing her both critical acclaim and widespread fame, especially in Germany. By 1981 her health had become very frail, and she wrote her last poem. Perhaps she had enough faith "in the poetry / that weaves humanity's / myth" ('Faith' p. 53) to know the answer to the question she had asked in 'When I Have Gone' (p. 111):

> When I go away
> from our forgetful earth
> will you speak
> my words
> a while for me?

She died in 1988.

Jean Boase-Beier & Anthony Vivis

When *Mother Tongue* was first published, in 1995, it was a monolingual book. Since then, Arc Publications' policy has been to present all their translated poetry as bilingual collections, as a way of signalling that original and translation should be seen together, even if not every reader can read both versions. When we came to revise the translation for this bilingual re-issue of the book, we realised that the presence of the original affects the translation in ways we had not expected. The main effect is on lineation. Though it was never our intention that our translations should be seen simply as English poems, we did take freedoms with line-breaks and divisions where we felt the English version demanded it. We often discussed the meaning of line-breaks when translating, and tried to capture in the English what we felt they meant, rather than echoing what they do. Now the translations will no longer be seen separately, but together with their originals, and so the shape of the poems has been adjusted to echo that of the originals more closely. That change has occasionally also required an adjustment to the English: 'The Net' (p. 23) is a case in point. The third stanza now matches in lineation the original and has become less compressed as a result.

But we have also made a few changes where we or our careful editor, Philip Wilson, felt the English read oddly, where there was unintended ambiguity (as in the original 'July', p. 57, which had "Your companion / swallows beneath her veil") or where ambiguity or understatement had been spelt out too clearly (as in 'The Unheard Heart', p. 57 where "beats in time" has become "keeps time").

Overall, the effect of the changes is to bring the translations very subtly closer to their originals.

A number of readers of the 1995 edition asked about our reasons for dividing the book into seven parts. Our main reason was to give order and shape to the collection, and the divisions are broadly thematic rather than chronological. For example, most of the poems in Part One are about language, those in Part Five about love and in Part Six they are about death. But these are by no means hard-and-fast categories, and the reader will no doubt see other connections. We have decided to preserve this intervention; it gives a sort of progression to the book which a selection from various sources might otherwise lack. We hope it will be deemed to be in keeping with the spirit of the book.

Jean Boase-Beier

ONE

EINHEITSSTAUB

Wir
Wortgewandte *(eloquent)*

gläubige Ketzer
Sternflieger
verliebt
in die Erde
die wir verbrennen
auf Scheiterhaufen

und singen Hymnen
auf den elektrischen Staub

Einheitsstaub
der uns aufbaut
abbaut

MUTTER SPRACHE

Ich habe mich
in mich verwandelt
von Augenblick zu Augenblick

in Stücke zersplittert
auf dem Wortweg

Mutter Sprache
setzt mich zusammen

Menschmosaik

DUST THAT JOINS

We
weavers of words

heretics who believe
we fly to the stars
in love
with the earth
which we burn to ashes
in cleansing fire

and sing hymns
to the electric dust

dust that joins us together
building up
breaking down

MOTHER TONGUE

I have changed
from myself into myself
from moment to moment

sprung into fragments
on the word path

Mother tongue
you piece me together

human mosaic

21

SPRACHE

Halte mich in deinem Dienst
lebenslang
in dir will ich atmen

Ich dürste nach dir
trinke dich Wort für Wort
mein Quell

Dein zorniges Funkeln
Winterwort

Fliederfein
blühst du in mir
Frühlingswort

Ich folge dir
bis in den Schlaf
buchstabiere deine Träume

Wir verstehn uns aufs Wort
wir lieben einander

DAS NETZ

Ich möchte etwas sagen
ein Wort
das alles sagt

Nicht
ich bin ich

WORDS

Keep me in your service
my whole life long
let me breathe in you

I thirst for you
drink you word for word
my source

Your angry glitter
winter-word

Lilac-fine
you bloom in me
word of spring

I follow you
even into sleep
spell out all your dreams

We speak the same language
we love each other

THE NET

I want to say something
one word
which says it all

not
I am who I am

23

nicht gebet mir
Funkeldinge Länder Geld

Das Wort
fällt mir nicht ein
ich falle
mir selber ins Wort

falle in ein Netz
aus zeitgeknüpften
Silbenmaschen

DIE ARCHITEKTEN

Ein Haus aus Phantasie
Gedankendach

Nicht
Wörter aus Silbenschaum

Frühling der mit Farben
um dich wirbt
die Schlagader des Sommers
in deinem Ohr
für dich blutet der Herbst
Erfinder des Winters so weiß
ist deine Einbildungskraft

Ja es gibt sie noch
Erbauer immaterieller Wohnungen

not regale me with
gemstones coins countries

The word
fails me now
My words
fall silent in me

fall into a net
with syllable-meshes
woven of time

THE ARCHITECTS

A house built of imagination
roof of thoughts

Not
words of syllable-foam

Spring courts you
with many colours
this Summer's artery
beats in your ear
for you Autumn bleeds
inventor of Winter
your vision so white

Yes they are still there
builders of immaterial dwellings

hinter Beton und Stein
errichten sie den Raum
für uns alle

ALS GÄBE ES

Als gäbe es
einen Himmel
und eine aufblickende
Erde

Als gäbe es
leuchtendes Blau
dumpfes Braun

Als gäbe es
Erdworte
überirdische Worte

Als gäbe es
Deinwort Meinwort
dich und mich

behind the concrete and stone
they create a room
for us all

AS IF

As if there were
heaven
and earth
looking up

As if there were
dull brown
and radiant blue

As if there were
heaven-words
and words of earth

As if there were
your words my words
you or me

IMMER DAS WORT

Wenn ich Gold sage
mein ich das Wort

Wenn ich Worte sage
meine ich
Gold Weltanfang Mensch

dich und mich
im Gespräch

SÄTZE

Kristalle
unregelmäßig
kompakt und durchsichtig
hinter ihnen die Dinge
erkennbar

Diese Sucht
nach bindenden Worten
Satz an Satz
weiterzugreifen
in die bekannte
unbegreifliche
Welt

ALWAYS THE WORD

When I say gold
I mean the word

When I say word
I mean
gold new world people

you and me
exchanging words

SENTENCES

Crystals
uneven in form
compact transparent
everything behind them
visible

This obsession
for binding words
sentence after sentence
to reach even further
into this known
unknowable
world

JENSEITS

Wir werden uns
wieder finden

du wirst
die begonnenen Worte
zu Ende dichten

Sprüche
für Hörende
jenseits aller Grenzen

ICH HALTE MICH FEST

Wer hat mir
den Regenbogen
aus dem Blick gerissen

Ich wollte ihn befestigen
an sieben Worten

Im Regen ertrinken
meine Augen

Ich halte mich fest
an einem Blatt
an diesem Papierblatt

BEYOND

We shall find
each other again

you will write
an ending
for words begun

sayings for those
who hear
beyond all bounds

I AM HOLDING FAST

Who has torn
the rainbow
from my field of vision

I tried to tie it fast
to seven words

My eyes are drowning
in the rain

I am holding fast
to the paper
this sheet of paper

LUFTSCHLÖSSER

Die Schwalben
sind ausgewandert
aus dem Kinderland

Ausgewandert
das Kinderland

Die Kinder
alt geworden

Ich
im Niemandsland
baue Luftschlösser
aus Papier

CASTLES IN THE AIR

The swallows
have gone away
out of the land of childhood

Gone
the land of childhood

The children
all grown old

I
in no man's land
build castles in the air
out of paper

TWO

PAUL CELAN

In hermetischer Stille
begraben
sein blutendes Wort
aus der Herzkapsel
gepreßt
von sternschwarzen
Flügeln getragen
entfaltet stechendes Licht
dessen Schatten ihn
schrecklich
erleuchtete

GEORG TRAKL

Melancholie
vorabendblau

Staubgeflüster
Im Schattenlaub
brechen Tiere zusammen

Der Herbst ist ein
goldener Kadaver

Wald
blutende Wunde

*

PAUL CELAN

Sealed
in hermetic silence
his word
squeezed bleeding
from the capsule of the heart
borne
on wings black as stars
releases blinding light
by whose shadow
he is cruelly
illuminated

GEORG TRAKL

Melancholia
twilight-indigo

A whisper of dust
In the leafy shadows
beasts fall to their knees

This Autumn is a
golden carcass

Wood
seeping wound

    *

Deine Wunde
heilt nicht
Georg

REGENBOGEN I

Himmelweite
Begegnung
zwischen Wasser
und Sonne

Sieben Farben
zusammengespannt
damit der Bogen
nicht breche

Hebt das Siebengespann
die sieben Todsünden auf?

MENSCHLICH II

Wenn man lang
in die Wolken blickt
sieht man oft
Ungeheuer und Engel

Georg
Your wound
has never closed

RAINBOW I

An encounter
wide as the heavens
between water
and sun

Seven colours
harnessed together
so that the bow
will not break

Can this team of seven
take away the seven deadly sins?

MYSTERY II

Look for a while
into the clouds
and you will often see
ogres and angels

Auch das Laub hat
viele Gesichter
Manchmal erkenne ich
einen Freund
im Blattwerk

So menschlich werden zuweilen
vertraute Dinge

Aber die Menschen
sind Rätsel
die ich lösen möchte

ERFAHRUNG

Erfahrung sammeln
in Wäldern Bergen
Städten

in den Augen
der Menschen

in Gesprächen
im Schweigen

The leaves too
have many faces
Sometimes I recognise
a friend
within their tracery

At times how human
familiar things become

But human beings
are mysteries
I am trying to solve

EXPERIENCE

Gather experience
in woods mountains
cities

in the eyes
of men and women

in talk
in silence

IDYLLE

In der Hütte
am entlegenen Ort
sind die Wände bemoost
die Namen verwischt

Im Hinterhof
kratzt der glückliche Hund
seine steile Unterschrift
in die Erde
und dreht sich dreht sich
atemlos
um den Atem
der Halme

MENSCHLICH

Im Fenster steht die Landschaft
sechs Häuser mit ihren
kleinen Gärten

Baumgespräche
die Pappeln grüßen
ohne sich zu verneigen

Man nahm sie ernst
und gab der Gasse
ihren Namen

Schnurgerade Wege wo
die Wasserbögen sich verschränken

IDYLL

In the hut
with moss-covered walls
in that isolated place
the names are hard to read

In the yard
a happy dog scratches
its sloping signature
into the earth
and turns turns turns
breathless
round the breath
of grasses

GAMES

In the window stands a landscape
six houses each with
its own small plot

Trees talk
the poplars say hello
without nodding their heads

Someone has taken them seriously
and given this lane
their name

Dead straight the paths
where arcs of water criss-cross

ein Gitter aus flüssigem Kristall

Ein- und Ausatmen
der Zeit und Jahreszeiten

Wir sind menschlich
uns freut das Spiel

ERWARTUNG UND WANDLUNG

Die Tage werden dünner
Auf Rostzweigen hängen
die Schwüre Verliebter
die sie vergaßen wie
Eichhörnchen das Versteck ihrer Nüsse
Oben wehen weiße Schleier
Vorhänge auf Fenstern aus Kobalt

Dunkle Laute kommen vom See
wo die Angst sich verborgen hält
unter der Wange des Wassers
Du hörst das heimliche Raunen
der Warnung und Wandlung
Gezähmte Felsblöcke warten
geduldig auf Metamorphosen
lächeln und ihre Silberzähne
kauen das Wetter
Halme bewahren noch ihre zarte Gestalt

a grid of liquid crystal

Time and the seasons
breathing in and out

We are human
we enjoy these little games

AWAITING TRANSFORMATION

The days are growing thin
From the mesh of branches hang
pledges spoken by lovers
and left behind like nuts
from the hoard of a forgetful squirrel
White veils waft overhead
curtains at cobalt windows

Deep sounds come from the lake
where fear lies hidden
under the cheek of the water
You hear the muted murmur
of threat and transformation
Domesticated cliffs wait
patiently for metamorphosis
they smile and their silver teeth
close on the elements
blades of grass still keep their fragile shape

ihr Eigenleben und den Zusammenhang
mit ihrer Rasse, dem Rasen

Schatten schaukeln die Parkbänke
Wind wiegt das schüttere Laub
Kinder lassen ihr Spielzeug liegen
laufen der Sonne nach
Luftballons kommen geflogen
in eifrigem Aufstieg
Sie halten sich wohl für Vögel
die Höhe für Heimat
und feiern ihr Steigen
Aeroplane mit tiefen metallnen Stimmen
rattern die unpersönliche Sprache
der Zweckmäßigkeit

Wieder tönt es vom See
mit verdichtetem Dämmerlaut
Wir erschauern
vor den Mahnrufen aus dem Wasser
und halten den Atem an
in Erwartung der Wandlung

LETZTE MUTTER

In Blut und Wasser geboren
erzogen im Urwald
der Großstadt

their own lives and the ties
with their own race, the turf

Shadows shake the park benches
winds sway the thinning leaves
children abandon their toys
to chase the sun
Then balloons appear
climbing eagerly
They seem to believe they are birds
the heavens their home
they celebrate their own ascent
aeroplanes with booming metal voices
rap out the anonymous words
of utility

Once again the lake echoes
with compressed twilight sounds
We shudder
in fear of the warnings from the water
and hold our breath
awaiting transformation

ESSENTIAL MOTHER

Born of blood and water
formed in the forest
of the city

Ein Dschungel grenzt
an den andern
durch Messer getrennt

Mit dem Lichtgipfel fliegen
im Giftfluß schwimmen

Letzte Mutter
Luft
wir bringen sie um

WÄHREND ICH ATEM HOLE

Während ich Atem hole
hat die Luft sich verfärbt
Laub und Gras trocknen in anderer Tonart
am Himmel hängt eine Fahne aus Stroh

Während ich Atem hole erfriert
in meinen Nerven eine Gestalt
ich höre den Umriß eines
Engels verklingen

Es ist Zeit den
Traum zu bauen in Grau
er ist ruhlos geworden und hat
sich schon niedergelassen in meinem
Haar während ich Atem hole

One jungle
borders upon another
divided by the knife

Flying high as light
swimming in the poison-flood

Essential mother
air
we are killing her

WHILE I AM DRAWING BREATH

While I am drawing breath
the air has changed colour
leaves and grass have dried in different tones
a banner of straw hangs from the sky

While I am drawing breath a figure
freezes to death in my nerves
I hear the silhouette of an
angel dying away

Now it is time
to form my dream in grey
it has grown uneasy and has
come to rest on my
hair while I am drawing breath

Inzwischen ist die Sonne verglast und
hat Sprünge bekommen. Ich suche ihre
unversehrte Form im Hudson aber
in seinen ergrauten Augen sind
die Konturen verschwommen
Vom Norden kommt eine
hurtige Hand und treibt
die Tropfen in den
Atlantischen Ozean
während ich Atem hole

SCHNEE

Schnee fällt
die Welt wird weiß

In der Sonne
glitzert das Weiß
in allen Farben

Weiße Sterne
blühn in der Luft

Am Horizont
hinter den Bergen
sieh Schneewittchen
und die sieben Zwerge

Nachts
ist das Weiß schwarz

Meanwhile the sun has glazed over and
sprung cracks. I look for its
flawless form in the Hudson but
in those greying eyes its
outlines are blurred
From the North there comes a
sudden hand which drives
the drops into the
Atlantic Ocean
while I am drawing breath

SNOW

Snow falls
the world turns white

In the sun
that white glitters
in every colour

White stars
blossom in the air

On the horizon
beyond the montains
look: Snow White
and the Seven Dwarves

At night
the white is black

51

wie die finstere Königin
hinter den Bergen

BEKENNTNIS

Ich bekenne mich

zur Erde und ihren
gefährlichen Geheimnissen

zu Regen Schnee
Baum und Berg

zur mütterlichen mörderischen
Sonne zum Wasser und
seiner Flucht

zu Milch und Brot

zur Poesie
die das Märchen vom Menschen
spinnt

zum Menschen

bekenne ich mich
mit allen Worten
die mich erschaffen

black as the dark queen
beyond the mountains.

FAITH

I profess my faith

in the earth and its
dangerous mysteries

in rain in snow
in tree and mountain

in that murderous mother
the sun in water and
the water's flight

in milk in bread

in the poetry
that weaves humanity's
myth

in humanity

I profess my faith
with all the words
that create me

THREE

JULI

In Dornenadern
das geklärte Blut
sonngesalbt

Auch Distelfinger
haben zärtliche Nägel
im Lerchenlicht

Hirsche halten
den Himmel
im Geweih

Wann trittst du
aus dem Gebüsch
Adam
deine Unsterblichkeit ist um

Deine Gefährtin
Schwalben im Hemd
wirft dir den Apfel zu
die Erde

DAS UNHÖRBARE HERZ

Im Geäder des Tags
schlägt das unhörbare Herz der Erdfee
die lautlose Trommel

Es begleitet die Spieluhr der Planetenpulse
die Nadeln der Sekunden

JULY

In the arteries of thorns
the cleansed blood
anointed by sun

Even the fingers of thistles
have delicate nails
in the lark-light

Stags hold
the heavens
in their antlers

When will you
emerge from the Garden
Adam
your span of immortality has ended

Your companion
veil full of swallows
throws at your feet the apple
earth

THE UNHEARD HEART

In the arteries of everyday
the earth fairy's unheard heart beats
its soundless drum

It keeps time with the musical clock of the planets' pulses
the needles of seconds

verwunden es nicht
Es ist gefeit
gegen Zeit und alle
Angriffe der Berührung

Manchmal wenn es sehr still ist
sehr weiß um mich
sehr anfänglich in mir
hör ich das unhörbare Herz
in meinem Atem
wie eine Uhr aus Luft
und die Musik der Spieldose
ist lebendig in meiner Schläfe
mit planetenhaft gedämpftem Ton

DER KUCKUCK ZAUBERT

Der Kuckuck im Laub
zaubert sein Ritual
mit geübter Zweisilbigkeit
Deutlich hört man seinen
magischen Mund den
Sommer beschwören

Die Wetterfee hält
im Ausland den Schnee gefangen
Sonnenlachen weiten sich
zu Seen wo Weiden baden
und Schwalben

cannot wound it
It is invulnerable
to time and all
assaults of contact

Sometimes when it is very still
very white all round me
very primeval within me
I hear the unheard heart
in my breathing
like a clock made of air
then the melody of the music-box
is alive in my temples
its tones muted like the moving spheres

THE SPELL OF THE CUCKOO

The cuckoo among the leaves
casts its ritual spell
in smooth two-syllable notes
Distinctly we hear
its magic mouth
calling the Summer

In foreign lands the weather-fairy
keeps the snow prisoner
pools of sun grow
into lakes where willows bathe
and swallows

Im Nest rührt sich das Ei
erwacht in Pans Arm
die Nachtigall

Der Mücken ephemeres Ballett
schreibt helle Kreise
aufs unverfängliche Luftblatt

DAS EINMALEINS

Die Gefangnen im Turm
halten den Wärter gefangen
und üben mit ihm
das Einmaleins der Stunden

Ins Wandgewebe
sind Labyrinthe gestickt
Irrgänge führen zum
Sesam-öffne-dich

Nachts holen die
Gefangnen verstohlen
die Welt in den Turm
verteilen sie regelmäßig
untereinander
Am Morgen ist alles
spurlos weggeräumt
die Zellen sind wieder
finstre Rechtecke
ohne Vögel und Wasserfälle

In the nest an egg comes to life
in Pan's arms
the nightingale wakens

A brief ballet of midges
draws bright circles
on the timeless page of the air

TIMES TABLE

The prisoners in the tower
have imprisoned their warder
and with him they recite
the times table of the hours

Labyrinths are embroidered
into the tapestry of the walls
passages leading nowhere
but to an Open Sesame

At night the prisoners
gather up the world in secret
bring it into the tower
divide it fairly
amongst themselves
In the morning every
trace is gone
the cells once again
gloomy rectangles
without birds or waterfalls

Die Gefangnen begrüßen sich
verstohlen
mit Weltabglanz
und üben mit dem Wärter
das Einmaleins der Stunden

HUNGER

Im Kerker
ich träume
den Apfel

Herr erlaub mir
die Sünde

(Aus deiner Rippe Eden
Adam aus meiner)

Blinder Blick
durch das Guckloch
Verstohlen pflanz ich
das Wort in der Zelle
beschwör den Apfel
zu wachsen.

Hinter dem Rücken
des automatisch wachsamen Engels
traumhoch
der Baum

The prisoners share
secretive greetings
tinged with the faint glow of the world
and with their warder they recite
the times table of the hours

HUNGER

In my prison
I dream the apple

Lord grant me
my sins

(Out of your rib Eden
Adam out of mine)

Blindly peering
through the peep-hole
Secretively I plant
the word in this cell
exhorting the apple to grow

Out of the angel's
limited line of vision
the tree
tall as a dream

Du grüner du roter
du bitterer
Tollkirschenbaum

KAMILLEN

Kamillen
Die grünen Jahre
bevölkert von Faunen und Feen
wuchern unter der Schläfe
Nymphen treiben ihr
Waldwesen weiter
im Raum aus Maschinen

Goldner Tee
In der Nische raschelt der Seidenrock
Engel halten den Spiegel
Ein Kinderchor unter dem Fenster
im Orchester
der Frösche und Grillen

Weltraum
überfüllt mit
Körpern und Katastrophen
Labyrinth der Länder
von Drachen bewacht
Rosen unwissend daß
ein Schatten auf ihnen lastet
der Rumpf des Robots

Apple-green cherry-red
deadly tree
of bitter nightshade

CHAMOMILE

Chamomile
The years of greening
peopled with fauns and fairies
run riot in my skull
And nymphs go on making their
forest mischief
in the machine room

Golden tea
A silk dress rustles in the corner
Angels hold up the mirror
A choir of children below the window
a symphony
of frogs and crickets

Universe
chockful of
corpses and catastrophes
labyrinthine lands
guarded by dragons
roses not knowing that
a shadow presses down on them
the rump of the robot

65

Laß fallen die Maske
Seifenblasen sprühn
von deinen Lippen auf
Minze und Mohn
der Flaum des Löwenzahns
schwebt überm See
Undine im Kelch einer Wasserrose
flüstert mit verschleierter Stimme
wie die Mutter
Freitag vor der Kerze

Elektrische Vögel
in Metallbäumen
kreischen dich wach
vom Daumen rollt der Ahnenring
mit dem Wappen der Linde
du legst an den Stahlkittel
dein Haar im Drahtlaub
fängt Antennen auf
in deinen Nüstern verflüchtigt
Kamillengeruch

NICHTS ÜBRIG

Vergib mir
Meer
ich kann nicht
schwimmen nicht tauchen
um deine rebellischen Märchen
zu finden

Let your mask fall
the soap-bubbles spray
from your lips on to
mint and poppy
the down of dandelions
floats over the lake
inside the cup of a water-lily
Undine whispers in a muted voice
like a mother on Friday
in front of the candles

Electric birds
in metal trees
screech you awake
the ring with its family crest of lime
rolls from your thumb
you put on your coat of steel
your hair in leaves of wire
picks up aerials
in your nostrils the scent
of chamomile subsides

NO OTHER WAY

Forgive me
sea
I cannot swim
on your surface or below
to find your unruly
legends

Es bleibt mir nichts übrig
als sie zu erfinden

IMMER ATLANTIS

Immer geht Atlantis unter
in unserm Hinausstaunen
immer ist's ein atmendes Grün
mohnendes Rot
Zypresse und Marmor
immer Feste in schaukelnden Gärten
ebenmäßige Menschen
immer die Heiligen Zarten Alleinleidenden

Sie steigen auf in uns
versinken in uns
wir sind ihr Grab
Immer im Schutt von Palästen
ist ihr Tod lebendig in uns
mit verwunschnen Zypressen
Schlangen und Paradiesen

Immer sind wir eingewoben
in den Glanz auferstandner
Städte und Reiche
immer spüren wir den Kristall des Erdballs
im Auge brennen
immer funkelt Atlantis
am Gestade unseres Herzens

There is no other way
but invention

ATLANTIS ALWAYS GLITTERING

Atlantis is always sinking
beyond our astounded gaze
it is always a breathing green
a poppied red
cypress and marble
there are always celebrations in swaying gardens
well-proportioned people
always holy and delicate and suffering alone

They well up in us
sink down in us
we are their tombs
And always in the rubble of palaces
their deaths are alive in us
with all the enchanted cypresses
serpents and Edens

We are always interwoven
with the radiance of resurrected
cities and empires
we can always feel the crystal of the earth
burning in our eyes
Atlantis is always glittering
beyond the shore-line of our hearts

FOUR

DEIN HAUS

Die Sonne sagt
schlaf dich wach
mein Kind
ich leuchte dir
heim

Der Regen
ich weine um die
verbrannten Kinder
mein Kind
weine mit mir

Staub
mit erstickter Stimme
mein Haus ist
dein Haus

NACH DEM KARNEVAL

Nach dem Karneval kamen die Magertage
mit Schimmelbrot und Bitterkraut
Mich hungerte nach Feigenfleisch
mich dürstete nach Apfelsinen

Mit einer Karawane ging ich
durch die Wüste auf Datteljagd
Der Sand stak mir im Hals
Der Rücken des Kamels
war meine Heimat

YOUR HOUSE

The sun says
sleep yourself awake
my child
I will light your way
home

The rain
I am weeping for the
children who played in the fire
weep with me
my child

Ash
choking on the words
my house is
your house

THE CARNIVAL OVER

The carnival over, the lean times came
the days of mouldy bread and bitter roots
I hungered for the flesh of figs
I thirsted for oranges

I joined a caravan and crossed
the desert on a date hunt
Sand stuck in my throat
A camel's back
became my home

Die Stunden waren Öfen um die Stirn
die Sterngebilde Kreuz und Skorpion

Am Morgen blühte rot am Horizont
die Fata Morgana die nicht näherkam
Nur einmal nahm uns eine Oase auf
das Wasser roch nach Feuer Mohn und Mond
Feigen und Datteln waren verdorrt

MÜHLEN AUS WIND

Das tägliche Brot
kommt uns teuer zu stehen

Mühlen aus Wind
mahlen Sandmehl

Am Rand einer Rinde
ernährt sich
die Not

Gib was du nicht hast
Liebe dem Nachbarn

Was suchst du
im flüchtenden Wasser
Narziß

The hours like ovens round my head
the constellations Scorpio and Crucifix

At daybreak the horizon grew red
with a mirage which would not come closer
Only one oasis gave us shelter
its water smelt of poppies moon and fire
its dates and figs had shrivelled up

MILLS MADE OF WIND

Our daily bread
comes at great cost

Mills made of wind
grind the grains of sand

Famine feeds
on the edge
of a crust

Give your neighbour the love
you have never had

What is it you are seeking
in the fleeting water
Narcissus

MIT DEM SIEB

Mit dem Sieb
schöpfe ich Wasser
für meine Mühle

halte die Flügel in Gang
mit meinem Atem

mahle
den Hunger

IN JENEN JAHREN

In jenen Jahren
war die Zeit gefroren:
Eis so weit die Seele reichte

Von den Dächern
hingen Dolche
Die Stadt war aus
unnachgiebigem Glas
Menschen schleppten
Säcke voll Schnee
zu frostigen Scheiterhaufen

Einmal fiel ein Lied
aus goldnen Flocken
aufs Schneefeld:
      "Kennst du das Land
        wo die Zitronen blühn?"
Ein Land wo Zitronen blühn?

IN A SIEVE

In a sieve
I scoop up water
to drive this mill

keep the sails in motion
with my breath

grind the meal
of hunger

IN THOSE YEARS

In those years
time was frozen:
ice as far as the soul could reach

From those roofs
hung daggers
The whole town made
of inflexible glass
people dragging
sacks of snow
to frozen funeral pyres

One day a song
of golden flakes
fell upon the snow-field:
        "Do you know the country
        where the lemons flower?"
A country where lemons flower?

Wo blüht das Land?
Die Schneemänner
wußten nicht Bescheid

Das Eis wucherte
und trieb
weiße Wurzeln
ins Mark unsrer Jahre

RAUCH

Diese gebrochene Säule
Rauch

So wanken die Säulen
der Griechentempel
in meinem Traum-Athen

Aus den Augen
der satten Menschenfresser
quillt Rauch
mein Wort ist schwarz geworden
davon

Ich schlucke bittere Pillen
aus Dreißigjahr-Rauch
meine Stimme erstickt
im Rauch des ewigen Gettos

What land flowers now?
The snowmen
did not know.

The ice grew thicker
sent down
white roots
into the marrow of our years

SMOKE

This fractured column
smoke

   And the columns tremble like this
in the Greek temples
in the Athens of my dreams

From the eyes
of sated man-eaters
smoke surges
and my words
have blackened
in it

I must swallow the bitter pill
of the smoke of thirty years
my voice chokes
in the smoke of the endless ghetto

in schönen
barbarischen Ländern

Lösch das Feuer Bruder
wenn keiner dir zusieht

UND MANCHMAL DER WIND

Nebel goldne Augen klagende Stimmen

Die Toten huschen Hand in Hand
durch den Nebel
durchqueren goldne Augen
ziehen Gassen
klagender Stimmen
entlang

Als noch alles zusammenhing
gab es ein schönes Geschlecht
das aufrecht ging
reine Umrisse hatte
Kreaturen die
Sterne begleiteten
Sonne erlernten
Erhaben waren die Tage
Muscheln und kleine Steine
hatten ewige Türen

in beautiful
barbaric lands

    Put out the flames brother
    when no one is watching

AND SOMETIMES THE WIND

    Fog golden eyes wailing voices

The dead glide hand in hand
through the fog
through watchful golden eyes
and pass
down alleys
of wailing voices

Before things fell apart
there was a beautiful race
walking upright
perfectly proportioned
creatures who
ran with the stars
mastered the sun
Those days were sublime
when shells and tiny pebbles
had doors to eternity

Jetzt ist alles verwischt
das Nebelhorn stöhnt
in die Ohren der Toten

Manchmal kommt ein Wind
der mit scharfen Scheren
den Nebel in Streifen schneidet
und dazwischen ist viel entzündetes Blau

Nebel goldne Augen klagende Stimmen
und manchmal der Wind

DAMIT KEIN LICHT UNS LIEBE

Sie kamen
mit scharfen Fahnen und Pistolen
schossen alle Sterne und den Mond ab
damit kein Licht uns bliebe
damit kein Licht uns liebe

Da begruben wir die Sonne
Es war eine unendliche Sonnenfinsternis

Now it is all confusion
and the fog horn moans
in the ears of the dead

And sometimes a wind comes
with keen scissors
cutting the fog into strips
between them stretches of inflamed blue

    Fog golden eyes wailing voices
and sometimes the wind

AND SHUT OUT THEIR LOVE

They came
with guns and jagged banners
shot down the moon and all the stars
and shut out their light
and shut out their love

That day we buried the sun
And there was eternal night

SCHALLENDES SCHWEIGEN

Manche haben sich gerettet

Aus der Nacht
krochen Hände
ziegelrot vom Blut
der Ermordeten

Es war ein schallendes Schauspiel
ein Bild aus Brand
Feuermusik.
Dann schwieg der Tod
Er schwieg

Es war ein schallendes Schweigen
Zwischen den Zweigen
lächelten Sterne

Die Geretteten warten im Hafen
Gescheiterte Schiffe liegen
Sie gleichen Wiegen
ohne Mutter und Kind

WEIDENWORT

Dem Strom
ruf ich zu
mein Weidenwort
gebeugt
am Ufer
aus allen Wurzeln blutend

STRIDENT SILENCE

Some saved themselves

And hands crept
out of the night
brick-red with the blood of those
they had murdered

It was a strident spectacle
an image formed of flames
music made of fire.
Then death fell silent
Fell silent

This was a strident silence
Smiling stars glinted
among the twigs

The saved wait at the harbour
Where the wrecked ships lie at anchor
Almost like cradles
without the mother and child

WILLOW WORD

I call out
to the river
my willow word
bowed
on the bank
from every root bleeding

aufgerissen
das Stück Erde
das mich hielt

Nächte
zusammengeschnürt
zu einer einzigen Nacht
im ehernen Schlaf
ich trinke
abstrakte Sterne
im Strom
mein Weidenwort
ruf ich zu
den Versunknen
die hinabtrieb
die Bö
zu den Steinen

EIN TAG IM EXIL

Ein Tag im Exil
Haus ohne Türen und Fenster

Auf weißer Tafel
mit Kohle verzeichnet
die Zeit

Im Kasten
die sterblichen Masken

and torn
the clods of soil
that held me fast

Nights
knotted together
into a single night
in an iron sleep
I drink
abstract stars
in the river
I call out
my willow-word
to the sunken souls
the squall has
driven down
to the pebbles

A DAY IN EXILE

A day in exile
a house without doors or windows

Time drawn on a tablet
charcoal
on white

In a chest
the mortal masks

Adam
Abraham
Ahasver
Wer kennt alle Namen

Ein Tag im Exil
wo die Stunden sich bücken
um aus dem Keller
ins Zimmer zu kommen

Schatten versammelt
um's Öllicht im ewigen Lämpchen
erzählen ihre Geschichten
mit zehn finstern Fingern
die Wände entlang

ARCHE

Im Meer
wartet
eine Arche
aus Sternen

auf die
überlebende
Asche
nach der Feuerflut

Adam
Abraham
Ahasuerus
Who knows all the names

A day in exile
when the hours stoop
to climb out of the cellar
and into the room

Shadows gathered
round the oil-lamp's eternal flame
tell their stories
along the walls
with ten dark fingers

ARK

On the sea
waits
an ark
of stars

for the
ashes
that survive
the flood of fire

ASCHE

Im Aschenregen
die Spur deines Namens

Es war
ein vollkommenes Wort

Feuer
hat es gefressen

Ich warf mein Staubgewand
in die Flamme

Hinter blindem Blick
deine Augen
ziehen mich an

DER NÄCHSTE APRIL

Daß ich dich wiederseh
im April
von Asche frei –
kann es sein?

Kaiserin Sonne
im Atemhemd
Baum ohne Angst
die Lerche real

Es ist nicht lang her –
ein Atemzug Geschichte

ASHES

In the rain of ashes
is the trace of your name

It was
a perfect word

Fire
consumed it

I threw my cloak of dust
upon the flames

Behind that blind gaze
your eyes
draw me to you

WHEN APRIL COMES

To see you once again
when April comes
free of ashes –
can it ever be?

The sun an Empress
in her cloak of breath
tree without fear
the lark so real

Not so long ago –
for history a mere breath

Wann in der Zeit aus Sprengstoff
dürfen wir dichten
am Strohlager?

Der antike Traum im Blut
blieb intakt:
Eden, Engel, du

Wird der nächste April
unversehrt sein?
Darf ich dich wiedersehn
von Asche frei
unter Versen?

But when in these days of dynamite
have we the right to write
on our beds of straw?

That ancient dream has stayed intact
within our bloodstream:
Eden, angel, you

Will this coming April
emerge unscathed?
Have I the right to see you once
again free of ashes
entangled in verses?

FIVE

IM FLUG

Im Flug
das Weite suchen

wo alle Wörter
verlorengehn

Worte finden
die dich lieben

HINTER DER HAUT

Du
morgens mittags nachts
ein anderer

Ich kenne dich
am Spiel deiner Augen

Du lächelst
sprichst und versprichst

Das Wort hinter deiner Haut
hat einen andern Ton

Man hört ihn nicht
ich höre ihn manchmal
hinter meiner Haut

ON THE WING

On the wing
you seek freedom

where words
have all been lost

you find language
which speaks of love

BENEATH MY SKIN

You
morning midday at night
a different person

I know you
from the movement in your eyes

You smile
you speak you promise

The words beneath your skin
have a different ring

Which cannot be heard
yet I sometimes hear it
beneath my skin

IN DIR

Über dir
Sonne Mond und Sterne

Hinter ihnen
unendliche Welten

Hinter dem Himmel
unendliche Himmel

Über dir
was deine Augen sehen

In dir
alles Sichtbare
und
das unendlich Unsichtbare

LIEBE III

Wir werden uns wiederfinden
im See
du als Wasser
ich als Lotusblume

Du wirst mich tragen
ich werde dich trinken

Wir werden uns angehören
vor allen Augen

IN YOU

Above you
sun moon and stars

Beyond them
endless worlds

Beyond the heavens
endless heaven

Above you
what your eyes see

In you
all that is
visible and the
endless invisible

LOVE III

We shall come together again
in the lake
you as water
I as lotus flower

You will carry me
I will drink you

We shall belong together
in the eyes of the world

Sogar die Sterne
werden sich wundern:
hier haben sich Zwei
zurückverwandelt
in ihren Traum
der sie erwählte

LIEBE

Erwacht
als Stimmen uns trafen

flogen Fische durch unser Haar
zartfarbig die Flossen
fast Blumen

Wasser schäumte herauf
aus begrabenem Brunnen
mit hohler Hand
schöpften wir
tranken einen Schluck
der Rest rann
durch die Finger

schöpften Mut
erfrischt
auf Jagd nach den Stimmen

über uns
immer noch sprachen sie

And even the stars
will stare in wonder
that there are two
who have changed back
into the dream
which chose them

LOVE

Awakened
as voices caught us

fishes flew through our hair
delicately coloured fins
almost flowers

Water bubbled up
from a buried spring
we collected it
in cupped hands
drank of it
the rest ran
through our fingers

drank new courage
refreshed
in pursuit of the voices

above us
still they spoke

sternmächtig
erschreckend

Wir legten uns
zu den Fischen
legten ab
jedes Wort

DIE INSEL

Als wir uns
auf der Insel trafen
waren Sonnen verwoben
zu einem Gobelin
in den der Atem des
Wassers geknüpft war

In der Staubzeit
rückten die Sonnen
auseinander
die Insel wurde ans Land geschwemmt
du lagst ein Goldfisch
im Glasbehälter

Auch diese Zeit schwand
Ich stricke den Strand
der Insel
ins Buch

strong as stars
frightening

We lay down
with the fishes
took off
all our words

THE ISLAND

As we met
on the island
there were two suns woven
into one tapestry
with the breath of
the water intertwined

In the days of dust
these two suns moved
apart
the island was washed ashore
like a goldfish you lay
in your glass vessel

Then these days faded too
Now I knit the island shore
back into
my book

SIX

ALTE ERGRAUTE FRAU

Im Zimmer voll nichts und voll niemand
sitzt sie beim Fenster Stunde um Stunde

Jenseits der Scheibe
ist die Welt ein Zusammen:
Häuser Bäume Wagen Menschen
Gebilde entstehen
verschieben sich
winden und binden sich
lösen sich bilden sich wieder
im großen Zusammen
jenseits der Scheibe

Die Scheibe lebt laut ihr Draußen
alle treten sie
treten über sie hinweg
aber sie lebt dreist
ihre Lautwelt aus Pfiffen und Stimmen

Ausgeschlossen vom Draußen
tritt die ergraute Frau
zurück ins Zimmer
voll nichts und voll niemand
Allein in der Kammer aus
Kalk und Holz
unter der mageren Sonne der Lampe
tut sie ihr winziges Werk:
die Arbeit der Hausfrau

Grau wie die Wand
ist ihre Angst
an den Geist genäht
grau der Saum
im Ohr ihrer Enge

OLD GREY-HAIRED WOMAN

In the room filled with nothing and no-one
she sits by the window hour after hour

Beyond the pane
is a world of contexts:
houses trees cars people
structures appear
shift
twining and joining
separating then forming again
in the vast context
beyond the pane

The pane lives out its world aloud
they kick it in
step right through it
but it lives out still
its defiant world of whistles and voices

Shut out from the outside world
the grey-haired woman steps
back into the room
filled with nothing and no-one
Alone in her small room
of wood and whitewash
beneath the frail sun of her lamp
she completes her tiny tasks:
the work of a housewife

Grey as the walls
her fears
are stitched to her mind
the hem grey
in the closed space of her ear

Die Wände weinen das Grau
der Wiederholung
Bett Tisch und Stühle
sind Fremde die sich befeinden

Der härteste Gegner der Spiegel
ist eisig bereit
sie aufzunehmen
im raumlosen Raum
sie zu halten im Bann
der erschreckten Augen
Kein graues Haar verschweigt er
keine Runzel
Sie schaut in ihr Schicksal aus Glas
und wundert sich daß es nicht bricht

SÄRGE

Gewohnt
auf den Schultern
Särge zu tragen
schwer
vom Abfall der Zeit

Dann ruh ich
hölzern
im Gras
das mich trägt
als wär ich
ein Sarg

The walls weep the grey
of repetition
bed table chairs
are strangers who have become hostile

Her harshest enemy the mirror
is icily ready
in the roomless room
to take her in
to hold her in the spell
of her frightened eyes
It conceals not a single grey hair
or wrinkle
She looks into her fate of glass
amazed that it does not shatter

COFFINS

Accustomed
to carrying coffins
on my shoulders
heavy
with the waste of these times

I rest now
wooden
in the grass
which carries me
as if I were
a coffin

SPANNUNG

Meine Haut
tätowiert
mit verworrenen Zeichen

Nachts
liege ich in einer Urne
da wohnt
die verbrannte Welt

Am Morgen öffne ich
die Augen der Sonne

Sie steht auf
und spannt mich
vor die Räder
der Uhr

WENN ICH VERGEHE

Wenn ich vergehe
wird die Sonne weiter brennen

Die Weltkörper werden sich
bewegen nach ihren Gesetzen
um einen Mittelpunkt
den keiner kennt

Süß duften wird immer
der Flieder
weiße Blitze ausstrahlen der Schnee

SIGNS

My skin
tattooed
with jumbled signs

At night
I live in an urn
in which lie
the ashes of the world

Every morning I open
my eyes to the sun

Which arises
and yokes me
to the cogs
of the clock

WHEN I HAVE GONE

When I have gone
the sun might burn still

The planets still move
to their own laws
round a centre
no-one knows

The lilac still smell
as sweet
the snow send out its white rays

111

Wenn ich fortgehe
von unsrer vergeßlichen Erde
wirst du mein Wort
ein Weilchen
für mich sprechen?

AUSTAUSCH

Wer kennt nicht
die Beruhigung der Sterne
wenn die Nacht
iIhre Träume abtritt
an unsern Schlaf

Schatten
Fische
Schaukeln im Fluß
diese Flut von Berührungen

Verschieden
sind die Formen
der Liebe
und Angst

wenn die Nacht
ihren Schlaf abtritt
an unsere Träume

When I go away
from our forgetful earth
will you speak
my words
a while for me?

EXCHANGE

Who has not known
the stars as calm as this
when night
gives up its dreams
to our sleep

Shadows
fishes
sway in the stream
the flow of sensations

The shapes
of love
and of fear
separate

when night
gives up its sleep
to our dreams

NACHT

Die Tulpe
schließt die Tür

Orions silberne Äpfel
sind reif

Die Quelle
wiederholt den Raum
aus Traum und Tropfen
mit genauem Laut

NIGHT

The tulip
closes its door

Orion's silver apples
have ripened

With crystal sounds
the fountain
recreates its shape
of dreams and drops

SEVEN

STILLE NACHT

Wer sagt daß ich singe
ich singe nicht ich sage
schön diese Nelke im Glas
atmet noch
das Märchen Vorbei

Schnee schon schwarz
unter dem Fenster
Stille Nacht vielstimmig
Wand hinter Wand

Auf diesem Blatt
der Schatten
ist meine Hand
sie schreibt die Nacht
ist ein Schatten mein Partner
drängt ich muß packen
meine Zeit verreist

MIT FRAGEN

Ich komme
mit Dornenfragen
blutarmer Sonne
Disteln und Wind

mit der Ameisenkönigin
und ihrem empörten Heer
mit Fragen woher wohin

STILL THE NIGHT

Who says I am singing
I am saying not singing
how lovely in its glass this carnation
as it breathes
the legend on its way

Snow now black
below the pane
still the night has many voices
walls beyond walls

Upon this page
the shadow
is my hand
writing the night
is mere shadow and my partner insists
I should pack
my time is going on a journey

QUESTIONS

I come with
thorny questions
bloodless sun
with thistles and wind

with the queen-ant
and her indignant army
with questions whither and whence

mit dem Hügel unterm Stein
mit zuckender Kerze
Talglippen
Fragen aus Qualm

mit der erwürgten Liebe
mit dem Scherben
von deinen Augen geraubt
darüber der Geierschrei

ich komme
zu wem
mit Fragen
warum wozu

AUF BARRIKADEN

Wir auf Barrikaden
immer
dreht sich der Erdball
mit uns revoltiert
gegen sich selber

Wir Erzväter Erzmütter
Urenkel
drehen die Zukunft
auf Barrikaden
aus Steinen
Worten
Blut

with the hill beneath the stone
with the flickering candle
lips of wax
questions formed of smoke

with strangled love
with the broken vessel
stolen from your eyes
the screech of vultures above

I come
to whomever
with questions
why and wherefore

ON THE BARRICADES

We on the barricades
endlessly
the globe turns and turns
joining our revolt
against itself

We patriarchs matriarchs
great-grandchildren
turn the future
on the barricades
of stones
of words
of blood

ROSE AUSLÄNDER was born Rosalie Scherzer in 1901 into a German-speaking Jewish family in Czernowitz in the Bukowina, then part of Austria-Hungary. After the First World War the Bukowina became part of Romania, and Rose emigrated to the USA in 1921 with her friend Ignaz Ausländer, whom she later married, but divorced after ten years. Ausländer's first book appeared in 1939, and she travelled between the USA and Romania until 1941, when the Nazis occupied Czernowitz, forcing Rose and her mother to live in the ghetto, and later in hiding. After the Second World War, when the Bukowina had become part of Russia, Rose Ausländer returned to the USA, where she wrote poetry only in English for several years. In 1965 she emigrated to Germany, and from 1972 until her death in 1988 lived in the Nelly Sachs House in Düsseldorf. From 1965 many collections of her poetry appeared, winning her a number of literary prizes.

JEAN BOASE-BEIER is a translator of poetry from and into German and is Professor of Literature and Translation at the University of East Anglia, where she runs the MA in Literary Translation. She has written many academic works on translation, poetry and style: recent publications include *Stylistic Approaches to Translation* (2006, St Jerome Publishing) and *A Critical Introduction to Translation Studies* (2011, Continuum). She has recently completed the research and public engagement project "Translating the Poetry of the Holocaust", funded by the Arts and Humanities Research Council. Jean Boase-Beier's poetry translations include Ernst Meister: *Between Nothing and Nothing* (2003, Arc Publications) and she is editor of the 'Visible Poets' and 'Arc Classics' series.

ANTHONY VIVIS, who died in October 2013, was a playwright and translator who played a leading role in introducing postwar German drama to the English-speaking world. A former dramaturg with the Royal Shakespeare Company and BBC Drama editor, he was best known for his translation of plays by dramatists such as Manfred Karge, Rainer Werner Fassbinder, Gerlind Reinshagen and Franz Xaver Kroetz. He collaborated on a number of translated poetry collections including *The Brontës' Hats* (1991, Reality Street Editions) by Sarah Kirsch, which he translated together with Wendy Mulford.

Also available in the series
ARC CLASSICS: NEW TRANSLATIONS OF
GREAT POETRY OF THE PAST
Series Editor: Jean Boase-Beier

FRANCO FORTINI
Poems
Translated from the Italian by Michael Hamburger

MARCELIJUS MARTINAITIS
The Ballads of Kukutis
Translated from the Lithuanian and introduced
by Laima Vince

VLADIMIR MAYAKOVSKY
Pro Eto – That's What
Translated from the Russian by Larisa Gureyeva
& George Hyde and introduced by John Wakeman
Complete with 11 photomontages by
Alexander Rodchenko, reproduced in colour.

ED. PETER ORAM
The Page and The Fire
POEMS BY RUSSIAN POETS ON RUSSIAN POETS
Selected, translated from the Russian
and introduced by Peter Oram

SALVATORE QUASIMODO
The Night Fountain: Selected Early Poems
Translated from the Italian
by Marco Sonzogni & Gerald Dawe

GEORG TRAKL
To the Silenced: Selected Poems
Translated from the German and introduced by Will Stone

RAINER MARIA RILKE
Pure Contradiction: Selected Poems
Translated from the German and introduced by Ian Crockatt

EMILE VERHAEREN
Selected Poems
Translated from the French and introduced by Will Stone

Further titles of poetry in translation are available in
'Arc Visible Poets', 'Arc Translations', 'Arc Anthologies' and
'New Voices from Europe & Beyond' (anthologies)

www.arcpublications.co.uk